IGNCA Rock Art Series-5

General Editor
Kapila Vatsyayan

Conservation of Rock Art

UNESCO Chair in the field of Cultural Development

Indira Gandhi National Centre for the Arts

IGNCA Rock Art Series-5

CONSERVATION OF ROCK ART

Edited by

Bansi Lal Malla

Indira Gandhi National Centre for the Arts

New Delhi

Aryan Books International

New Delhi

ISBN-81-7305-149-6

First Published 1999

Publishers:
Indira Gandhi National Centre for the Arts
Central Vista Mess, Janpath, New Delhi-110001

Aryan Books International
Pooja Apartments, 4B, Ansari Road, Darya Ganj
New Delhi-110002

Printed in India at B.B.N. Printers, New Delhi

Contents

Foreword

DENOTING the archaic expressions surviving in the form of paintings, drawings, and engravings on the caverns, rocks or boulders, the rock art is often bracketed with prehistory for the purpose of study and research. Attempts have also been made to view it within a chrono-frame in the context of antiquity and inferences have been drawn to associate it with prehistoric and later cultures. In the present context what is interesting to mention is that with several sections of people in Africa and India and elsewhere rock art continues to be a living tradition, although in the wake of ever expanding global modernity its survival is facing the danger of disappearance in the course of time. Besides, in many countries especially those of Asia and Africa there is a lack of arrangements for the proper preservation of ancient rock paintings, petroglyphs, boulder engravings, etc. Even in developed nations like France to prevent damages to the painted surfaces on account of rising tourism the original under-ground caverns containing paintings at Lascaux have been closed to visitors a few decades back. Only scholars are permitted to see the paintings with especial precautions, under a special permit. However for the tourists, who visit Lascaux in large numbers, the French authorities have successfully made an exact copy of this actual rock structure in the close vicinity of the original site with exactly similar paintings. A famous painted prehistoric cave in Spain is also stated to have been fully closed to preserve paintings therein. Elsewhere, in countries like India rock art is also threatened owing to modern developments like construction of dams, roads, etc. which often result in loss of ecology, rise in moisture, blasting of rocks, etc.

In view of such developments, the Indira Gandhi National Centre for the Arts (IGNCA), which is deeply involved in the study and documentation of rock art, felt the necessity of holding a discussion amongst the specialists on the preservation and conservation of rock art. As a sequel, a seminar on the subject was held in February 1996 in New Delhi to consider and discuss the issues relating to the preservation of rock art.

The present publication brought out under the IGNCA's Rock Art Series contains the papers presented during the seminar by the participants who are well known experts on the rock art in India. Preceeded by an introduction giving the background of rock art studies in IGNCA, it includes articles on conservation, preservation and maintenance of rock art sites, conservation techniques and long term planning, analysis of pigments of painted caverns and their preservation, management of two foremost rock art sites in India, and requirements for conserving and managing rock art remains and cultural dimensions of rock art. The publication 'Conservation of Rock Art' although is not a bulky volume, it concentrates, perhaps for the first time in India in recent years on the vital problem of preserving the rock art remains which of course requires much extensive studies and research.

I am grateful to the contributors to this monograph, especially scholars, viz., Prof. V.H. Sonawane, Dr. B.B. Lal, Shri B.N. Tandon and Shri B.M. Pande besides my esteemed colleagues in the IGNCA Prof. B.N. Saraswati, the principal organiser of the seminar and

Dr. Bansi Lal Malla, the editor of this publication. I also take this opportunity to thank Dr. Kapila Vatsyayan, the Academic Director of IGNCA without whose vision and encouragement it may not have been possible for the institution to take up studies on rock art and bring four well received publications on the subject, viz., *Rock Art in the Old World* (ed. Michel Lorblanchet), *Deer in Rock Art of India and Europe* (ed. G. Camuri, A. Fossati, Y. Mathpal), *Rock Art in Kumaon Himalaya* (Yashodhar Mathpal) and *Rock Art in Kerala* (Yashodhar Mathpal).

I hope the present monograph, despite its small size, will inspire the younger generation of scholars to take up research on the preservation of rock art, a vitally significant subject.

M.C. Joshi

List of Illustrations

1

Introduction

Baidyanath Saraswati

ONE of the major academic programmes of the Indira Gandhi National Centre for the Arts (IGNCA) relates to exploring artistic manifestations emanating from man's primary sense perceptions. The programmes of *Ādi Dṛṣya* (primeval sight) and *Ādi Śravya* (primeval sound) have initiated several projects in the visual and performing arts.

Rock art forms a crucial component of the *Ādi Dṛṣya* programme, but *Ādi Dṛṣya* is not equal to prehistoric rock art. The IGNCA's conceptual plan aims to open the doors to the realization that rock art is pure and absolute and hence capable of dispensing great experience beyond its original culture and time.

Any conceptual plan is always provisional in the sense that it is only a hypothesis to be tested. A good theory of rock art is a model gallery devised by a meaningful correlation between the construction of concepts and the interpretation of designs. While a new theory is always an extension of the previous one, its crucial confirmation lies in the disapproval of the method that survives. If the existing method is found inconsistent with the concept, then it has to be abandoned or modified. The IGNCA rock art research programmes will seek to test this generality.

The first and the foremost task of the IGNCA Rock Art Gallery is to raise a data bank and to provide infrastructural facilities. The seven steps so far taken and to be taken in this regard are summarised as follows:

1. *Compilation* of cross-cultural bibliographical information on rock art within and outside India.
2. *Collection* of water-colour reproductions, photographs, slides and other visual texts on rock art.
3. *Field studies* leading to the discovery of new rock art sites in India.
4. *Computerization* of visual and textual data, allowing efficient storage and retrieval possibilities and high resolution (such as CD-Rom or video-discs).
5. *Work station* complete with equipment for all potential users. Facility for interactive, user-friendly programme for cross-cultural data-scan and study.
6. *Developing* an expert system through in-house research as an aid for the users carrying out higher studies.
7. *Network* with other centres of display and research work on rock art. Cultural institutions with primary data on rock art will be provided a network.

As rock art is a relatively young discipline, various avenues of growth are being explored and its research is being carried out in a universal context. Studies have been conducted in Kumaon Hills in Central Himalaya, Jhiri in Central India and Kerala in South India. A major field project has been launched, within the Indo-French CEP, in collaboration with Professor Michel

Lorblanchet and his team. Two sessions of fieldwork (recording and conservation study) have been done in Jhiri during December 1993 and January 1996. Water-colour recordings and two trial excavations have also been done.

Under the aegis of Unesco, a workshop on "Development and Application of Expert Systems in Lifestyle Studies" was organized in 1991. The focal point was an "expert system" developed jointly by a subject specialist of rock art and a knowledge engineer, with a view to explore the impact and applicability of the AI techniques to cross-cultural studies.

With Unesco's support, a Global Conference on Rock Art was held in 1993, where eminent scholars from sixteen countries had gathered to present their findings. The first of its kind in Asia, this conference held nine sessions, thematically organized as follows: 1) Understanding rock art in a universal frame; 2) Country report; 3) Cross-cultural comparison; 4) Environment, management, conservation and documentation; 5) Classification, chronology and standardization; 6) Consideration of context; 7) Form, content and interpretation; 8) Artificial Intelligence and rock art research; and 9) The world gallery of rock art.

Following the Global Rock Art Conference, the exhibition *Mṛga* (Deer: Early Images) was designed in 1993 in collaboration with Dr. Angelo Fossati, an Italian specialist in rock art. The exhibition focused on the comprehension of nature and life through line-and-colour in time and space. It revealed the continuity of the deer motif in Indian and European rock art traditions.

A three-day meeting of Experts on Conservation, Preservation and Management of Rock Art was held in IGNCA from 1 to 3 February 1996, under the aegis of Unesco. It aimed at: *discussing* the extant theories of rock art; *examining* concrete cases for the conservation, preservation and management of rock art caves and shelter; *identifying* conservation hazards and interventionist practices; and *suggesting* national policies for rock art management. The essays collected here refer to this meeting.

2

Conservation and Preservation of Rock Art in India

M.C. Joshi

Background

INDIAN specimens of rock art, illustrating several varieties of painted, engraved or crudely carved forms created by human hand in the past on the rocks, boulders or stone surfaces in different areas were generally known for over a long period to the people of a locality where such remains were situated, although their archaeological importance was brought to light much later in modern times. Yet, the painted or engraved forms constituting rock art were hardly regarded as art expressions, particularly in the context of India, till the early decades of the present century. In this connection, we may like to mention that Alexander Cunningham, the father of Indian archaeology, who saw copies of rock paintings from Chargul in Mardan district of North Western Frontiers province (now in Pakistan) dismissed them as boyish sketches. However, the local people, in many cases in India regarded these unrefined forms as sacred to the extent that some of the shelters were treated by them as holy spots or as shrines. It is on this account that we notice some kind of continuity of rock art tradition amongst certain sections of Indian society, particularly, in the areas where their specimens are found. In a way the local beliefs thus also helped in a few cases in the preservation of, atleast, some sites.

Despite discoveries of painted rock-shelters over a hundred years ago in the sub-continent and later, the subject did attract very few explorers. In fact the issue was not considered to be of much importance by most archaeologists of yore and other scholars for a long time, although some interesting studies were carried out by a limited number of researchers on the painted rock-shelter or engravings. In pre-Independence India, rock paintings and petroglyphs and even their suggested pre-historic or later antiquity did not inspire the authorities of the Archaeological Survey of India or other similar bodies to undertake detailed exploration or even documentation of rock art.

Limited Protection

The main reason for ignoring the study or investigations on rock art by official Indian archaeologists and its analysis was the strong historical and indological base of early archaeological studies in India. Thus little attention was paid to even known painted rock-shelters or to their systematic and detailed documentation and exploration of new areas containing rock art. The position however improved in post 1947 period when scores of new rock art sites were discovered and even excavated and detailed studies were undertaken and published. Yet, the conservation and preservation of rock art sites still remains a neglected issue for various reasons and even the protected rock shelters are rarely attended to.

Out of numerous notable specimens of rock art available in India, only a few have been brought under Central Government's protection like Pachmarhi caverns or those at Hoshangabad (M.P.), and some of painted shelters in the undivided district of Mirzapur in Uttar Pradesh, and latest addition being the famous rock art centre at Bhimbetka near Bhopal. Except the last named site, where in recent years some good maintenance work has been undertaken by the Archaeological Survey, nothing has been done in respect of other rock art sites. Several decades back a little work of chemical preservation was carried out at Hoshangabad and Pachmarhi but Mirzapur shelters continued to remain ignored. The State Governments may also have protected some shelters in their areas but, to the best of my knowledge, no serious attempts for their preservation seem to have been taken up.

It may thus be observed that very limited number of rock art sites have been subjected to conservation and resultantly they are exposed to the danger of getting damaged to the extent of loss of features of art specimens and in certain cases the remains are stated to have been even got destroyed beyond recognition either by human or natural agencies as there was none to take their care. In recent years, it came to my notice that in Ladakh area some boulders bearing interesting Buddhist and other engravings were broken and even blasted for collecting stones for constructional purposes. Today it is difficult even to identify the sites which contained the lost engraved boulders. There is also no detailed account of all the rock art sites in the country. Besides, in some cases even locations of the painted caverns have been forgotten.

Problems of Conservation

We are not in a position to blame one single Indian agency for such a sad state of affairs in respect of the preservation of the rock art for varied reasons. The painted shelters and engraved boulders are located in isolated spots and outlandish places which are not easily accessible. In comparison to pretentious monuments like Ajanta, Ellora, Mahabalipuram, Sanchi, Khajuraho, Konarak, Hampi ruins, Qutab Minar, Fatehpur Sikri or Taj Mahal or even secondary monuments or sites the rock art remains are considered to be most unimpressive and unsophisticated by the general public. In addition there is little knowledge amongst even the educated about the richness of the contents of rock art and its continuous tradition in village India. They also do not present any tourist attraction. Bhimbetka, being close to Bhopal, can be treated as an exception. Consequently, the Governments whether Central or State never thought of protecting and preserving examples of rock art in a larger scale.

What is needed now to look into the problem to suggest measures for the lasting survival of painted shelters and other specimens of rock art. The issue has to be viewed in totality for better preservation of the sites under reference. Broadly, this could be solved by attempting the following measures systematically:

1. Documentation
2. Developing methodology of Conservation, and
3. Environmental preservation

Thus the first step for proper identification and safeguarding the rock art remains located in little known areas, at least for the purpose of future referencing, is to compile a detailed and illustrated inventory of rock art in accordance with their situation in a state or region. Such a work should include all the known sites and their art and archeological contents. Bodies like the Archaeological Survey and Department of Anthropology, Government of India, should serve as nodal agencies in such a project. Universities and State Departments of Archaeology and other qualified learned institutions could be assigned a specific area containing rock art sites to collect and document the available data which may be later on published in instalments. The work can also be undertaken as a project under the University Grants Commission or the Indian Council of Historical Research. If possible Unesco aid could also be solicited for the purpose.

The conservation of rock art remains have multiple problems because of the diversities of medium. The sites comprise shelters and engraved or incised boulders or isolated rock surfaces in sandstone, in a few cases in quarzite, gneiss or slate and even granite in diverse environments and ecozones. The principal problem of conservation is faced by a painted rock shelter, especially in sandstone zones, is the presence of cracks, fractures and fissures damaging the paintings due to growth of vegetation and percolation of water inside creating moist conditions. The process of natural weathering of the rock and inherent weak rock fabric also serve as decaying agent for the painted surfaces. Most dangerous, however, are overhanging mass of projecting rock on the upper part of a shelter which can collapse due to adverse natural factor or even human vandalism especially blasting of boulders in the vicinity of a site due to constructional requirements at times. Attempts should be made to fill up the cracks and fissures in the shelter from within and outside and to make the top and sides of the cavern watertight by using suitable material like coloured cement or lime, depending on the nature of a stone surface, mixed with powdered parent rock or proper type of sand and desirable chemicals wherever necessary. In carrying out such works it has to be seen that the material foreign to rock has to be tested before its application and it has to be used in way matching with the original surface of the rock. To divert the flow of rainy water from entering inside, suitable channels or slopes may be provided on sides of a shelter. Undesirable vegetation should be periodically removed from within and top of a cavern. Further to prevent the overhanging rock projections from falling, strong masonry support even by using RCC could be provided by giving it a naturalistic rock form matching with the features of the shelters. But it must contain a date on its less conspicuous part indicating that it is an artificial support.

For the preservation of significant engraved boulders, if absolutely essential to arrest decay, suitable structures could be raised over them. Similarly canopied–frames could be provided on vertical rock faces containing carvings for their protection.

Along with structural conservation, rock art remains have also to be subjected to chemical treatment for proper preservation. However, application of chemical preservatives has to be made only after proper scientific investigations and minutest examination of the rock surfaces have been conducted before the treatment is commenced. For the use of a specific variety of chemical on a rock, it has to be subjected to proper tests in relation to its applicability on a particular rock or boulder in order to see its positive or negative reaction thereon. Through chemical preservation accretions from the painted surfaces could be removed, weathering of rock could be prevented and disintegrating of rock could be consolidated to a considerable extent. With the employment of chemicals on painted surface it is also possible to detect precisely the existence of more than a layer of paintings.

What is most desirable from the standpoint of conservation is to maintain natural conditions and original environment of the rock art sites. The trees, hedges, etc. growing around a shelter should be removed only when that is absolutely necessary in the interest of the better preservation of the remains. Further, as far as possible, no vehicular movement should be permissible within a rock art site and the pathways provided therein should look like natural jungle tracks. Similarly, if it is felt necessary to raise a fencing around one or more painted shelters, it must match with the environment and set up of the rocky elevation of the area and should be in the form of naturalistic hedging. In case the enclosure surrounding a site has to be in some kind of masonry, it should not look like a formally built wall and bear such features which tally with the local landscape. Besides, no modern construction should be raised in the close vicinity of any rock art site and if for security reasons it is found essential to build a residential structure, it should be of modest proportion and constructed in a style matching with rocky outcrop at the site.

Display of Reproductions

In order to familarize the general public with the importance of rock art of India and to encourage studies and investigation thereon, there is desirability to display reproductions of important examples of rock paintings and rock engravings, etc. in all the important museums, especially, the regional museums. In areas like Bhimbetka and Panchmarhi (M.P.), Mirzapur and Sonabhadra districts (U.P.) or Rachi-belt and Ladakh, it is desirable to establish exhibition centres in the neighbourhood of the shelters or district towns so that notable rock art reproductions of the nearby localities could be displayed in their local context. Such a measure is likely to inspire school children to learn something about rock art. The management of such centres could be given to some local agencies like Zila Parishad, Municipal Boards, Panchayats and even to Non-Governmental Organizations.

Preservation of the Art Tradition

India is amongst few countries of the old world wherein there is some sort of continuity of rock art tradition in certain areas like parts of Uttar Pradesh, Ladakh, Ranchi area of Bihar and elsewhere in various media. It is on account of the existence of such a tradition certain rock shelters also bear less than century old painting or engravings bearing palm impressions, conventional geometric designs, age old symbols and other sacred forms, stylized figures, etc.. Archaeologists may not allow such a continuity, in the context of a rock art site for this may amount to disturbance in the antiquity of the art. Yet, for the survival of this rich art legacy, the continuity of the tradition connected with this ancient art needs to be preserved in even a modified form. Therefore, the people living close to rock art sites may not only be permitted but should be encouraged to draw paintings on unpainted rocks and engrave unengraved and unincised boulders or rock surfaces located close to this habitat.

Safeguarding the Rock Art Sites

Due to diversely located large number of rock art sites in the country it may not be possible for the central or State Government to protect all of them. It is therefore, suggested through display centres, schools, colleges and local bodies, villagers and other interested citizens may be involved in looking after the rock art sites in their districts, villages or towns and areas in different parts of the country. Some of the local people, may take upon themselves the responsibility to inspect rock art sites, periodically, provided they are made to understand the significance of the rock art, in their neigbourhood.

Epilogue

In the foregoing paras we have attempted to discuss issues connected with the conservation and preservation of Indian rock art sites. In the context we have also done some exercise, which is, however, purely theoretical, in regard to suggesting some solutions of the problems. The validity of our suggestions could be proved only when it is possible to make their application in the area of rock art by the concerned agencies and individuals. I would, therefore, be grateful if scholars on the subject, prehistorians, anthropologists and archaeologists make it possible to assess our suggested solutions and offer their critical comments on the issues involved so that it is possible to improve the position.

Select Bibliography

1. Cockburn, J., "On the recent existence of *Rhinoceros Indicus* in the North-western Provinces", *Journal of Asiatic Society of Bengal*, Vol. 52 (1883), No. 2, pp. 56-64
2. Francke, A.H., "Notes on Rock Carvings from Lower Ladakh", *Indian Antiquary,* 31, 1902, pp. 398-401.
3. Ghosh, M., "Rock Paintings and other Antiquities of Prehistoric and Later Times", *Memoirs of Archaeological Survey of India*, No. 24, 1932, Calcutta.
4. Gordon, F.H., "Indian Cave Paintings: The Rock Paintings in the Mahadeo Hills" in *IPEX*, 1935, Berlin - Leipzig, pp. 107ff.
5. Lorblanchet, M., *Rock Art in the Old World*, (Ed.), Indira Gandhi National Centre for the Arts, New Delhi, 1992.
6. Mathpal, Y., *Prehistoric Rock Art of Bhimbetka*, Abhinav Prakashan, New Delhi, 1984.
7. Mathpal, Y., *Rock Art in Kumaon Himalaya*, Indira Gandhi National Centre for the Arts, New Delhi, 1995.
8. Mathpal, Y., *Rock Art in Kerala*, Indira Gandhi National Centre for the Arts, New Delhi, 1998.
9. Neumayer, E., *Prehistoric Indian Rock Paintings*, Oxford University Press, Delhi, 1983.
10. Tiwari, R., *Rock Paintings of Mirzapur*, U.P. State Archaeology Department, Lucknow, 1990.

3

Conservation, Preservation and Maintenance of Rock Art

V.H. Sonawane

ROCK ART is one of the richest cultural resources in the world which depicts the earliest expressions of human beliefs and ideas. It is associated with the cultural values, particularly in countries like India and Australia, where this art is a part of the living cultural heritage of its native population. This invaluable resource is at continuing risk everywhere because of the natural agencies like wind, water, insects, vegetation and human activities associated with farming, industry, tourism and other developments. Therefore, a professional level course to train persons to understand the causes of deterioration of rock art and to conserve, preserve and manage it, has been overdue (Pearson 1991:104). Looking at the seriousness of the issue, at the very outset, may I congratulate the authorities of the Indira Gandhi National Centre for the Arts for coming forward to organize meeting of experts of such kind to discuss various issues related to conservation, preservation and maintenance of rock art as a first step to overcome the Indian situation, in particular, and the world, in general.

The heritage of Indian rock art is one of the world's longest unbroken tradition and hence the concepts pertaining to its vital cultural role are still very much alive. An adequate conservation strategy would not only recognize the importance of our cultural legacy, but also develop a sensitive and complementary approach to its protection. In India, we are at a stage now when most of the paintings are deteriorating at an alarming rate, no matter whether they are on sandstone or on granite, and if proper measures are not taken at right time there would be an irreplaceable loss on the part of our rock art heritage.

The demand for conservation of rock art on a worldwide basis has been recognized by the Getty Conservation Institute (GCI) and Unesco has indicated a need for training in conservation of rock art in accordance with the priorities given by the organization to the preservation of world heritage, realizing rock art as one of the underdeveloped areas of conservation. I am glad to know that as a part of its priorities, Unesco has extended support for this deliberation in Delhi for the same cause. In India, where the rock art sites are far-flung in remote areas, sometimes in inaccessible parts of the country, no centralized authority either at State or Central Government level can cope with this herculean task without involvement and support from outside, at least to begin with initially.

Protection of rock art sites is itself an important task, and hence proper conservation through technical discipline based on combination of humanistic and scientific knowledge that contributes to prolonging the life of rock art is most essential. The rock art conservator requires not only a sound training in conservation theory and procedures but also a good understanding of sciences like geology, petrology, hydrology and chemistry.

In India, currently, we do not possess an integrated system of rock art preservation and site management, except a little effort very recently made by R.C. Agrawal of Archaeological Survey of India in the Bhimbetka complex of Central India as a first positive step (Agrawal 1994). France and Australia are the only two countries in the world which are currently advancing beneficially in the area of rock art conservation, preservation and site management. However, the ideas, methods and principles applicable at the Upper Palaeolithic cave sites of western Europe, especially France and Spain are in most cases unrelated to the Indian conditions because of their specific environmental setting. But the situation in Australia, as Bednarik has rightly pointed out, is extremely similar to that of India. Climate and geology of the vast majority of painted sites are similar or almost identical (Bednarik 1994:6-7a). Therefore, considering the near identical situation of Indian and Australian rock art sites, it is most appropriate that Australian experts should be consulted to minimize the experiments by sharing their experience on Indian soil.

Rock art sites have been located in the most diverse geographic and geologic regions of the Indian subcontinent having divergent climatic zones. This diversity in natural habitats of rock art paintings naturally causes adverse effect on their state of preservation and hence it is very difficult to treat them in a generalized or common effective manner. From the experience of several scholars who have been working in this field since long, one could learn that local environment played a very vital role either in favour or against the conservation threats received by the art forms. Therefore, it is very important to preserve the natural environment of the rock shelter areas as far as possible. When speaking of environmental preservation, one has to emphasize the need for maintaining the total ecological balance in the rock shelters housing paintings or any other art forms. The existing environmental conditions, therefore, should not be disturbed in any case. The immediate surroundings of rock shelters are important for the preservation of rock art.

In general it is observed that conservation threats to rock art sites can be broadly classified into two basic types: natural deterioration and human interference. Bednarik, because of his long association and commitment towards the rock art studies, could see that these two types cannot be always effectively separated. He says, a factor of natural deterioration may be sometimes indirectly attributable to human modification of the environment (Bednarik 1994:32).

The most significant danger of natural deterioration of Indian rock art comes from water seepage, surface flow and in some localities the capillary moisture. During monsoon season, rain drops throw up dust which settles in the already humid lower parts of the rock walls inside the shelters. And it is exactly these parts of the shelter that generally show a thick layer of opaque patina which obscures all traces of paintings. The patinae are vulnerable to the growth of lichens, fungi and other micro-organism which in turn make the under surface of painted rocks weak attributing damage to the painting. Similarly, most of the paintings are exposed to direct sunlight causing damage to them. It is believed that if they are still visible after so many hundreds of years, the sun should not affect them now.

But such damages are basically due to the recent cutting of trees and foliage rendering the shelters bare. Like sunlight, high winds also affect the paintings drastically. Many paintings which now look unicoloured were originally done in polychrome, mostly in red and white. While the red colour could withstand the ravages of time, white has remained in traces only. In a few very well protected spots, original polychrome paintings survive in good state of preservation indicating well maintained ecological balance since past to present. Paintings on granite surface seem to be less durable unlike paintings on sand-stone.

Animals and insects also cause considerable damage to the rock shelters and paintings executed therein. Because of human encroachment over the vast land, some wild animals and birds now take shelter in these less inhabited hilly tracts. They find these rock shelters more safe and damage the paintings. The devastating effects of termite, warp nests built over the pictures call aloud the need of protection by taking various measures for their proper conservation. Deforestation has threatened many rock art sites. Cutting of trees eliminates a protective shelter and exposes the art to rain, sun and aeolian erosion. At the same time, forcing wild bees too occupy rock shelters, which otherwise construct their hives on trees. The wax of the bee-hives melts in summer and drips on the rock paintings and thereby damages the art work (Tyagi 1991:28). Some of the above cited possible threats to rock art appear to be natural factors but apparently they are humanly caused factors by modifying natural environment against the code of conduct.

The sites which are easily accessible attract the attention of the masses. The possibility of damage to such sites from human vandalism becomes a real threat. On many occasions, it has been observed that visitors tend to destroy or damage major portions of painted shelters with paint, chalk, charcoal and even by engraving, indicating name, signature, date and other details. Sometimes, original pictures are found disfigured by repainting.

Much of human intervention is of recent origin. Some shelters are inhabited by forest dwellers who cook their food inside the shelters. The resultant smoke thus contributes serious damage to the paintings. Initially, some rock paintings were also seriously affected by the rock art researchers themselves, by using water spray techniques either for photography or sketch, outlining of features in the same colour for better results and even flaking of painted rock surfaces for obtaining colour pigments just out of curiosity. I suppose, nobody does this vandalism now; I mean the rock art researchers.

It is a matter of great regret that quite a few of such sites in recent years are being increasingly destroyed by mining for construction materials. Until recently, mining was done on a small scale by hand quarry but nowadays, most of the hills of rock art potentials are being mined using dynamite blasting in an unscientific and uncontrolled manner (Neumayer 1993:30).

The natural environment in which the rock art has managed to survive now depends on our moral responsibility to create an awareness amongst the masses for its proper conservation which nature has kept alive. For effective management, irrespective of its level, the awareness aspect has to be given utmost priority and particularly for the sites which are lesser known and are susceptible to vandalism. Education at all levels is certainly recognized as one of the corner- stones in protecting and conserving of rock art treasure. Our priority should not restrict to preservation of rock art sites simply as an aura of antiquity but should react as Australian aborginals look at their ancestral paintings with spiritual power. Conservation in the modern perspective constitutes the preservation of static images for all times, while conservation from Indian perspective means visible and tangible continuity of the spiritual content of the image or figure as a concept, *Ādi Dṛṣya* of IGNCA.

References

1. Agrawal, R.C. 1994. "An approach for the conservation of Bhimbetka", *Purakala,* Vol. 5, Nos. 1-2, December, pp. 25-30.
2. Bednarik, R.G. 1994a. "Some suggestions for the management of Bhimbetka, *Purakala,* Vol. 5, Nos. 1-2, December, pp. 5-24.
3. Bednarik, R.G. 1994b, "Rock Art Conservation in Australia", *Purakala* Vol. 5, Nos. 1-2, December, pp. 31-40.
4. Neumayer, Erwin 1993, *Lines on Stones—The Prehistoric Rock Art of India,* Manohar, New Delhi.
5. Pearson, Colin 1991, "Graduate Diploma in Conservation of Rock Art", *Rock Art and Posterity—Conserving, Managing and Recording Rock Art,* Eds. Colin Pearson and B.K. Swartz, Jr. Occasional AURA Publication No. 4, Melbourne, pp. 104-8.
6. Tyagi, G.S. 1991, "Conservation of Indian Rock Art", *Rock Art and Posterity—Conserving, Managing and Recording Rock Art,* Eds. Colin Pearson and B.K. Swartz, Jr. Occasional AURA Publication No. 4, Melbourne, pp. 28-29.

4

Conservation Technique and Long Term Planning for Preservation of Rock Art in Tropical Countries

B.B. Lal

ROCK paintings and engravings found in rock shelters and natural caves and caverns in different regions of the Indian subcontinent represent the earliest example of cave-dwellers' art. This art, sometimes described as primitive, marks an early style in the evolution and growth of Indian civilization. The finds of numerous rock art sites in different regions by the middle of the present century led Gordon[1] to observe that "Very ancient rock paintings have been discovered in Europe, and yet more, many of which were held to be very old, had been found in Africa. Without doubt it was now the turn of India to be included as a centre of palaeolithic art." In fact, during the past five decades a very large number of rock paintings have been discovered in different parts of India, and most of these rock art sites—rock shelters and natural caverns-have been found associated with microlithic industries, and some even with palaeoliths. Granules of red ochre—haematite-have sometimes been found in the floor deposits of certain rock shelters. Hunting is the main theme of these paintings; other interesting themes are: honey-collecting, dancing and musical instruments, use of fire and pot-making. Besides vehicles with—and without wheels, some scenes of worship are also depicted, the objects and symbols being trees, forests, besides trident, wheel (chakra) and Swastika. Whether the latter paintings depicting these symbols can actually be associated with the hunting-food-gathering folks of the Late Stone Age, as has been done by some workers,[2] is a question which merits a very careful scientific study. Mostly monochrome, these rock paintings have been described as primitive or prehistoric, and some of them are palaeolithic bearing affinities and comparison with the palaeolithic cave art of Cogul. Although guesses have been hazarded by scholars regarding the origin, development and chronology of this rock art, the actual dating of these rock paintings by scientific methods, such as radiocarbon dating or magnetic dating of associated pottery, or its thermoluminescence dating, is yet to be carried out. This rock art is thus not yet dated on internal evidence. Dewdney's[3] work in this regard is very interesting.

Geographical Distribution of Rock Art Sites

As regards the geographical setting[4] of rock shelters and caverns, it is seen that most of them are found in rocky, hilly and forested regions of Bundelkhand and Baghelkhand, constituting a part of the Kaimur range of the south of the Ganga. The central tableland of Madhya Pradesh, constituting Central India, is studded with rock art sites, and many painted rock shelters have been discovered in the Vindhyan region. In fact, a broad belt of microlithic sites associated with rock shelters and caves lies stretching across Central India along the Narmada and the Tapti rivers. Herein are located Carlleyle's painted rock-shelters at Rewa, Banda and Mirzapur, which provide important and interesting and extensive material, on which the earliest studies of Indian rock art were originally based. The rock shelters of Singhanpur and Kabrapahar, besides those at Hoshangabad and Pachmarhi in the Mahadeo hills have yielded considerable important material for the study of this early rock art. Rock-painting sites have also been found at Varanasi, Allahabad and Agra in the Ganga and the Yamuna valleys of Uttar Pradesh. Some of the painted rock shelters in Mirzapur district of Uttar Pradesh constituted the first group of Indian rock art sites to be copied and documented in detail more than six decades ago.[5] They are: Bhaldharia, Bijayagarh, Kohber, Lekhania, Likhunia, Mahararia and Ronp. Lekhania rock shelters in Mirzapur district were also studied in detail. They are particularly important because of finds therein of several human skeletal remains.

The important rock-painting sites in Madhya Pradesh, apart from those already described, are: Katni in Jabalpur district, Bairagarh and Shamala hills in Bhopal district, Gwalior hill in Gwalior district, Bijori in Narsinghpur district, Itar Pahar in Rewa district, Brijpur in Panna district, Chibbar Nala, Mori, and Sitakhardi, all in Mandsaur district, Bhinyapura and Kesalpura in Sehore district, besides Kharwai and Bhimbetka, both in Raisen district. Of these, Bhimbetka, about forty-eight kilometres from Bhopal, is a very rich rock-painting site, lying on a high ridge in the forest-clad Vindhyan range, comprising about 630 rock shelters and natural caves, of which about 500 carry numerous rock paintings.

There are hardly any significant finds of rock-art sites from north-east India, West Bengal, Bihar and Orissa. In the Deccan also, not many rock-art sites have been discovered so far. It is likely that extensive exploration in the rocky terrains in these regions may bring to light rock art sites comprising paintings and petroglyphs. Vast areas in these regions of the Indian subcontinent still constitute almost a blank so far as rock paintings are concerned. It is unlikely that the present paucity of rock-art sites in these region is an indication of the operation of unfavourable environmental and ecological factors in ancient times that prevented the growth and development of this art. Rather, it seems from past experience that intensive exploration and fieldwork in ecologically favourable regions, such as hilly tracts and forested areas near water bodies, like lakes and rivers, where essential needs for human existence, viz. raw materials for fabricating tools and implements, food and water, were at hand, would bring to light many rock-art sites. It may be mentioned that the rock paintings at Sitabhenji[6] in district Keonjhar, Orissa, have gone straight on the rough undulating under surface of the holocrystalline biotite granite rock boulder called "Ravanachhaya" without any preparatory work of smoothing it by plastering and priming. Only a thin limewash application was given to the bare, uneven undulating under surface of the boulder, perched on another rock boulder jutting out of the ground. Only red, yellow, white and black pigments are discernible. The only difference between these paintings and the rock paintings under discussion appears to be in the way the colours were applied; the paintings in rock shelters and natural caves generally show the figures and designs in outline only, whereas the paintings at Sitabhenji show the entire surface painted in colours-red, yellow, white and black, and mixed colours like polychrome mural paintings in rock-cut caves. These remarks apply equally well to the Jogimara rock paintings in Ramgarh district of Madhya Pradesh, where the paintings have gone straight on the unplastered rock surface. In point of technique and style and theme and subject matter, these two rock shelter paintings in Orissa and Madhya Pradesh respectively are entirely different from the murals in rock-cut caves, temples and other structural monuments, dating from the 2nd century B.C. to later times.

In the Deccan, some rock-art sites have come to notice in Chittor and Raichur districts. Further, some rock engravings i.e. petroglyphs, have been reported from Kapgallu in Benekal forest of Bellary district, and from Eddakal cave in Wainad district.

It is noted that most of the painted rock shelters and caves are located near river banks. Generally, these rock shelters of early man were located at sites where three essential requirements for survival, viz. food, water and raw materials for fabrication of his tools and implements, could be met. In fact, they are mostly situated on rocky outcrops on elevated ground, which commanded a panoramic view of the region, and provided the hunting-food-gathering rock-shelter dwellers with vantage points strategically important for hunting.

The rock paintings and petroglyphs described above constitute a rich cultural heritage. They are located in those regions of the Indian subcontinent which abound in sandstone and quartzite. The substrates of these rock paintings are thus the sandstone and quartzite, and no painting has been found on limestone, slate or shale.

The vast rock art of India has posed complicated problems of preservation, conservation and maintenance. Some of the rock shelters are extremely difficult of access, and their exploration has proved hazardous, as was experienced years ago at Singhanpur rock shelters, when some explorers, attacked by infuriated honey bees, had to run for miles to safety. In the absence of adequate facilities and safeguards, scientific study of rock shelter paintings has not made the desired progress, and the conservation needs of these works of art have not been fully attended to. Only a limited amount of work has been done so far for elucidating the causes of deterioration of the painted rock shelters located at easily accessible sites such as Adamgarh quarry, Hoshangabad, Doroathy Deep rock shelter and Bania Beri cave, both at Pachmarhi, besides some Bhimbetka rock shelters. The paintings at these sites have also been chemically treated and preserved. Besides, some rock paintings in Mirzapur district have been generally studied and scientifically examined for studying their materials and techniques for determining the causes of their deterioration. The materials and techniques which were employed in their execution have been studied by carrying out detailed examination and laboratory investigation of representive samples of rock and pigments. The environmental and ecological factors involved in the mechanism of degradation and deterioration of these rock shelters and caves and the paintings therein have also been considered.

Materials and Techniques

The rock paintings, executed in the form of drawings and outlines of figures, patterns and designs without general colouring of the background, show for colours—

red, yellow, white and black, as well as their mixtures. Green is rarely present, and there is no trace of blue. The paintings have gone on rock faces-vertical, near-vertical and horizontal and sometimes on curved surfaces, and on the under surfaces of projecting or overhanging rocks.

The rock engravings and petroglyphs, which constitute another form of rock art, have not been considered in this study, for no pigments have been used in their execution, and the support or ground on which they occur in sandstone or granite—the rock painting substrate, which has been examined chemically and microscopically as part of the study of the painted rock shelters.

Support and Ground

The paintings have gone straight on unplastered, unprimed rock surfaces, which were neither smoothed, nor dressed or polished before painting. Chemical analysis, spot tests and microscopic examination have established the use of red ochre for red colour, yellow ochre for yellow, white clay for white and charcoal for black. The red and yellow pigments are seen at places to have diffused into the rock, and permeated into the rock to a measurable depth. The colours were evidently used in liquid form, and not in powder form.

Pigment Medium

Minute pigment particles, lifted from the painted outlines at suitable spots, were subjected to chemical analysis and microscopic examination for establishing the presence of gum, glue, oil or resin. No binding medium could, however, be found in the pigment samples. This failure to establish the presence of any adhesive in the samples so examined, however, does not disprove the use of some organic binding medium. Such organic binding adhesives for the pigments used in the rock paintings are not likely to survive for long periods under hot and humid, and tropical and sub-tropical climatic conditions, and it is not unlikely that under the impact of adverse environmental conditions, both non-living and living, such adhesives of organic origin as glue, gum, resin, oil or fat or mucilaginous plant extracts suffered degradation and decomposition due to prolonged exposure to sun, wind and rain. In fact, bio-deterioration caused by bacterial activity and cryptogamic growth, chemical decomposition and autoxidation would have brought about total or near total destruction of the organic binding medium, and would not have allowed this organic matter to remain preserved in situ. The question whether a binding medium was used with the pigments thus still remains unresolved.

In this connection, it would be interesting to refer to the scientific investigation of the problem of binding medium in rock paintings in Australia, Siberia and Canada.

Medium in Australian Rock Paintings

According to McCarthy,[7] the colours were mixed in powder form with animal fat in locations where water was scarce, and in Arhem Land, the colours were mixed with orchid juice, a fixative used for the ground colour of paintings. However, Lommel[8] has opined that the fading and flaking observed in Australian Wandjina rock paintings, executed in mineral pigments comprising red and yellow ochres and white clay, besides ground charcoal, all mixed with water alone, is due to absence of a binding medium. Whether the presence of organic adhesives as binding media in pigments used in Australian rock paintings has actually been proved by scientific examination, or whether the use of such adhesives has been inferred from the current practice of aboriginal artists, is not clear from the literature.

Medium in Siberian Rock Paintings

According to published literature, some rock paintings in western Siberia were painted with red ochre mixed with blood. These paintings were studied by Chernetsov,[9] but details of the scientific work done on the adhesive are not known. Tests for the organic content in the pigment—blood or some other organic matter-have been inconclusive.

Medium in Canadian Rock Paintings

In connection with the study of rock paintings in the Canadian Shield Woodlands, Dewdney[10] has observed that any binding medium mixed with the pigment must have come from such organic materials as egg yolk, animal grease or fish oil, and that it cannot be said with certainty whether the organic adhesive had remained unaltered in situ in spite of prolonged weathering involving physical erosion, and mechanical disintegration of the substrate, chemical alteration of minerals, and bio-deterioration of organic matter, and whether remnants of the adhesives were available for radiocarbon dating of the rock paintings. Nor is it even certain, says Dewdney, that all paintings contained such binders in their pigments, in their original state. His experimental work on the durability of the pigments containing organic binders has yielded very significant results. He painted several figures on fully exposed and extremely rough granite blocks with the same pigment—mineral haematite-variously mixed with glue, oil and varnish; in two cases, no binder was used in the aqueous suspension of red ochre. After an exposure of twenty-four months, it was noticed that the paintings with the glue binder had almost vanished, but those with no binder, although clearly more impaired than others with oil or varnish medium, remained clearly discernible. Dewdney concluded therefrom that given protection from the more erosive weathering agents, a rock painting without any binder might last a long time.

That aqueous suspensions of ochreous clays—red ochre, yellow ochre and white clay-containing no organic binding medium can get firmly bound to rough bare rock surface, exposed to sun, wind and rain sprays, has been amply demonstrated by large-scale work of preservation and conservation of the weathering khondalite rock of the Sun Temple, Konarak situated in the hot and humid region of the eastern coast of Orissa within about two kilometres of the sea, not very far from the Lord Jagannath Temple at Puri. The results of these experiments have already been reported, and they show that aqueous suspensions of ochreous clays—red and yellow ochres and white clay-containing no organic binding medium, when applied to bare rough rock surface adhere so tenaciously that after a few years' exposure to hot and humid environment, they become completely resistant to sun, wind and rain, and even gentle abrasion of the rock surface with fibre brushes and cotton wool fails to dislodge the pigments. It seems probable, in view of the field data from Konarak experiments, that in most cases of Indian rock shelter paintings, the pigments were ground in water without incorporating any binding medium, and then applied to bare rock to produce the paintings. There is a fair degree of permeation of these aqueous pigments into the fabric of the rock, and the bond between the two is remarkably firm. Further it is probable, though not proved, that the slow action of water on the siliceous rock resulted in the formation of colloidal silica[11] and the latter produced on insoluble imperceptible layer on the pigments, thereby fixing them firmly to the rock substrate, and rendering them largely resistant to the weathering effect of sun, wind and rain.

Status of Indian Rock Paintings

Many rock paintings have suffered damage and deterioration on account of prolonged exposure to sun, rain and dust-laden winds. The rock surface has spalled and flaked away from sizeable areas, and many paintings have been damaged by erosion. Parts of rock shelters have fallen down on account of continued weathering and physico-chemical disintegration of the rock. Patination of the rock surface is also in evidence at many sites, but no desert varnish is seen. Although wind erosion is noticeable on many exposed areas, rock surfaces with desert varnish have not been encountered anywhere so far. The painted surface generally presents an all-round weather-beaten appearance on account of prolonged exposure to atmosphere, and the paintings located in comparatively sheltered parts of the rock caves and shelters are found covered with copious amount of wind-blown dust, grime, cobwebs and insect nests. Beehives have also been found in and near rock shelters. To this large-scale damage must be added the deliberate vandalism perpetrated by stray wayfarers, who lit wood and grass fires inside the painted caves and rock shelters. The smoke and tarry matter so generated settled on the painted surfaces and heavily stained the paintings. Chalk and charcoal marks left on the painted surfaces by unscrupulous visitors have in many cases caused much damage. In fact, this unscrupulous activity of vandals, who write and even engrave on the painted surfaces has done much to damage and even deface these artistic works of great cultural value.

Causes of Deterioration

From the status of the rock paintings[12] defined in the foregoing discussion, it is evident that the causes of their deterioration are many and varied. It is, therefore, essential that these causes of degradation and damage are dealt broadly with reference to three main elements, which constitute these paintings. They are: the carrier (rock or substrate), the pigments and the binding media. The behaviour of these elements or components has been studied with reference to the ambient environment of the rock shelters. Because of adverse environmental conditions (high temperature about 30C and above and high relative humidity for several months of the year, with violent and wide fluctuations), dust-laden winds, and considerable cryptogamic growth, such as moss and lichen, the substrate has been deteriorating and disintegrating because of the weakening of its texture, and appreciable chemical weathering. This has led to peeling and cracking of the rock surface, with concomitant loss of the pigments. Where the rock surface remains wet on account of rain sprays or seepage and percolation of rain water, there is considerable growth of moss and lichen, and paintings have suffered much damage on this account. Water soluble salts have also been responsible for damage in some cases. Paintings have also deteriorated on account of depredations of insect pests such as the formation and deposition of their nests, wax and carcasses. The main causes of deterioration of these paintings in rock shelters and caves are as follows:-

1. Physical disintegration and chemical weathering of stone of the painted shelters and caves.
2. Formation of cracks in the rock surface carrying the paintings.
3. Splitting, spalling and erosion of the painted surface.
4. Seepage of rain-water into the caves and shelters.
5. Cryptogamic growth such as moss and lichen.
6. Accretions of smoke and tarry matter from fires burnt inside the painted caves and rock shelters.
7. Growth of insect nests and hives on the painted surface and other areas.
8. Accretions of wind-blown dust and grime, cobwebs, and excreta of birds and bats in some cases.
9. Chalk and charcoal marks, and occasional engravings made by vandals.

Chemical Treatment and Preservation of Paintings

Limited fieldwork of cleaning, preservation and conservation of some rock shelter paints has been carried out at a number of sites. The details of the methods and materials employed in this work have been published by the author. To recapitulate some salient points it may be stated that there are seven rock shelters at Adamgarh quarry in Hoshangabad district, and the rock is quartzitic sandstone of pink colour. The floor deposits of these shelters have yielded a very large number of microliths, such as worked blades and lunettes. All the paintings in these rock shelters have been subjected to elaborate chemical treatment and preservation. The work of conservation has been documented by photographing the paintings both before and after cleaning and preservation. Drawings of the paintings have also been prepared. The consolidation of the painted surface was carried out and preserved. Drawings of the paintings have also been prepared. The consolidation of the painted surface was carried out with 3-5% solution of polyvinyl acetate in toluene containing 2% dibutyl phythalate as a plastisizer. The spraying of these ochre rock paintings has produced satisfactory and acceptable results, as proved by their good state of preservation several decades after treatment. The doubts expressed by Moore regarding the efficacy of this treatment have been found to be unjustified. The use of polyvinyl acetate as a surface fixative and consolidant of painted rock surfaces has stood the test of time. Paintings in Pachmarhi rock shelters-Dorothy Deep and Bania Beri cave—have also been conserved in the same manner.

Documentation of Rock Shelter Paintings

The two methods used in the documentation of this rock art are: tracing and line drawing to scale and photography in black-and-white and in colour. The problem of documentation of rock paintings has been discussed by several workers, but no agreement has been reached regarding the most suitable method of recording all the essentials. Tracing coupled with detailed photography would appear to constitute, as opined by Vinnecombe, the most accurate method of recording so long as a pre-scientific method of documentation is not available. The method of documentation adopted at Hoshangabad and Pachmarhi rock shelters is the best available at present.

Conclusion

To conclude the foregoing brief account of the study and conservation of the vast cultural heritage of Indian rock art, it may be observed that the work done so far has been totally inadequate and vigorous and sustained efforts are urgently called for undertaking a detailed and comprehensive survey, scientific study and conservation of rock shelter paintings at all recorded sites. It is, therefore, necessary to draw up an integrated plan of protection and management of all rock art sites with the following objectives:

1. Preparation of inventory or rock art sites with details of location of rock shelters, status of rock paintings, and problems of conservation.
2. Chemico-petrographic examination of substrates of paintings, pigments, binding media, and techniques of execution.
3. Detailed documentation for recording all significant features.
4. Systematic chemical treatment and preservation of paintings, and structural conservation and stabilization of caves and shelters.
5. Demarcation of rock art sites with walls and fencings, and prominent display of the prescribed *Protection Notice Board*.
6. Display of *Notice Board for Visitors* with the following request: *Protect this Heritage. Take nothing but pictures. Leave nothing but footprints.*

References

1. Gordon, D.H., *Prehistoric background of Indian Culture*, N.K. Tripathi (Private) Ltd, Bombay, 1958.
2. Gupta J., *Pragaitihasik Bharatiya Chitra Kala* (Hindi), Prehistoric Indian Paintings, National Publishing House, Delhi.
3. Dewdeny, S., 'Art and Archaeology Occasional Paper,' No. 24, Royal Ontario Museum 1970:20-21.
4. Lal, B.B., "Rock Paintings of India—A Study in Conservation", *Conservation in the Tropics*, IX, 1976, pp. 13-17.
5. Ghosh, M., *Memoir, Arch. Surv. Ind.,* No., 54.
6. Lal, B.B., "Preservation of Mural Paintings", *Ancient India.* No. 22 (1966), pp. 93-94.
7. McCarthy, F.D., *Australian Aboriginal Rock Art*, 1962 (2nd Ed), 35.
8. Lommel, A., "The Rock Art of Australia", in *Art of the World: The Art of the Stone Age*, Methuen, London, 1961, pp. 206-7.
9. Chernetsov, V., *Naskalnye Isobrazheniya Urala*, Moscow, 1964.
10. Dewdeny., *op.cit.*
11. Taylor, J.M., Wainwright, I.N.M. *Bulletin of the American Institute for Conservation.*, Vol. 14, 1974, No. 2, pp. 28-43.
12. Lal, B.B., "Indian Rock Paintings and their Preservation", in *Aboriginal Antiquities in Australia* (Ed. F.D. McCarthy), 1970, pp. 139-46.

5

Some Ancient Pigments and Problems in their Preservation

B.N. Tandon

THE tradition of murals has been strongest in India, says Shivaramamurti. Illustrations on board, canvas and wall all have a common-tradition and if miniature paintings are introduced, they look as if these have been taken and reduced in size from the walls. The ancient painter had a deep and sound knowledge about the nature of various colours. He was not only a master-artist but also a master executor and he had the future survival of his renderings in mind when he started to draw the paintings and, therefore, he used those colour ingredients which were permanent and durable.

India possesses a large number of rock-cut caves, temples, monuments, churches and even private *hawelis* which are embellished with murals. Some have survived the vagaries of age and time while other although important, have faded out into oblivion and only literary, evidence remains as source material. It is a well known fact that even prehistoric man tried to put down in line and colour some of their concepts in the form of animals and human figures and has left it to us to draw our own conclusions from the pictorial depictions. Some of the earliest indications of such paintings have been located at Adamgarh, Raigarh, Hoshangabad, Bhimbetka (M.P.), Chakradharpur in Bihar and Mirzapur in U.P (Carllyle in 1867). A few years back another group of rock paintings dating back to prehistoric-times was reported at Alamia railway station near Kota in Rajasthan. The colour used is red and the theme is animal figures in these rock-shelters. They might be linked with Bhimbetka. Similarly Fowcett in 1892 wrote about the existence of prehistoric rock pictures near Bellary in south Karnataka. Cockburn also published about some of the prehistoric paintings in the new Imperial Asiatic Quarterly Review in 1899. History of the pigments probably began with the civilization itself. Through analytical procedures it has been concluded that only those colorants were used which were cheaper and readily available. These were mainly oxides, carbonates, carbon and mineral in origin, having different chemical behaviour. Europe is not different. In that part of the world, the earliest cave paintings are from Lauscaux (15000 BC) in south France and Altamira in Spain. Altamira's bison paintings were red and black painted over protuberances in the rock-ceilings. These projections control the contours of animal bodies and supply a third dimension. The figures are engraved and painted as well and some parts even scraped to obtain the effect of light and shade. Most of the colorants especially carbonates, carbon black, etc., lamp black as Puch came into use very late in 14th–15th century AD.

Wakankar in his book on Stone Age paintings mentions that white pigment had been made from kaolin or limestone. There are exceptions also as at

Pachmarhi of black and purple obtained from magnesium oxide. In Bhimbetka copper compounds were used to produce bright shades of green, but a great majority of the paintings were done with haematite or oxide of iron to produce colour in red, yellow, orange or brown. These are all available as a surface. No evidence of binding medium is available at the prehistoric level. During Kushan period, the style continued to be the same. However, search for better techniques and materials continued. The theme of most such paintings was hunting and dancing scenes, cows and other animals.

In neolithic period—say 6000 BC or so—we find modifications from only pigments to tempered pigments as in Mesopotamia in which glue and gelatin has been reported.

During Mohenjo-daro and Harappan period, we have painted drawings on potteries. These were in the form of flowers and animals. The colour theme was red, black, yellow and white. All these confirm their mineral origin. This period was followed by descriptions of paintings in Ramayan and Mahabharat. Jogimara cave with murals is another example of importance (2nd century, BC) in M.P.

In the historical period; we find some most important examples like Ajanta having murals ranging from 2nd century BC to 7th century AD, Ellora paintings (7th century AD), Bagh cave murals (7th century AD), Pannamalai (7th century AD), Kancheepuram (7th century AD), Sittanavasal (9th century AD), Tanjavur (11-12th century AD), Armamalai Jain temple (9th century AD), Hampi and Leepakshi (16th century AD). Most of these paintings have been analysed in respect of their colorants and their technique determined.

These were in general tempera or Scceo. Lac dye has been reported from Bagh. Most of the colours detected were minerals as indicated below in case of Ajanta.

1.	Red	-	Red ochre
2.	Yellow	-	Yellow ochre
3.	Green	-	Glauconite
4.	Black	-	Lamp-black
5.	White	-	Kaolin and chalk
6.	Blue	-	Lapis lazuli

Somewhat less readily available than the ochres and earth colours were coloured minerals of heavy metals which were used at a late period. These are realgar, orpiment, cinnabar, malachite etc. An American chemist Gettens analysed some pigments from Bamiyan (5-8th century AD) and compared the results in terms of affinities of colorants and techniques, as follows:

1.	Red	-	Red lead
2.	Blue	-	Ultramarine
3.	Yellow	-	Ochre
4.	Green	-	Chrysocolla
5.	White	-	Calcium-sulphate
6.	Black	-	Charcoal black

The difference is very clear. In Ajanta the red colour is red ochre while in Bamiyan it is red lead. The green is a glauconite white. In Bamiyan it is chrysocolla. Further, Dr. Coomaraswamy in his paper on Technique and Theory of Indian Painting has mentioned the use of following pigments:-

1. Red - Cinnabar
2. Yellow - Orpiment and ochre
3. Black - Lamp-black
4. Blue - Indigo and ultramarine

As far as the technique is concerned Paramashevan showed that rough mud plaster was common to Ajanta, Bagh, Bamiyan and Kizil while rough lime plaster was common in Sittanavasal, Tanjavur, Conjeevaram. Ground of Ellora is mud, lime plaster or both. The fine layer of Bamiyan/Kizil is of gypsum. In Ajanta, Bagh, etc. it is a mixture of lime and small traces of gypsum.

Dr. Lal has analysed about 30 samples from Bamiyan (5-8th c. AD) and has compared the results in respect of technique and ingredients with Miran, 4th century AD analysed by Church, Kizil (Gettens) and Tung Huang (Gettens). In Bamiyan he found:

1. Black - Carbon black
2. Red - Red and yellow ochre
3. Yellow - Red and yellow ochre
4. Blue - Lapis lazuli
5. White - Gypsum
6. Green - Chrysocolla

Absence of azurite malachite has been noted. In case of Tung Huang, vermilion has been reported along with white lead mixed with ultramarine to produce blue and madder for orange red. The green is malachite. Thus it becomes evident that the Indian painters used yellow ochre, red ochre, carbon, lime and their presence is not only witnessed in Bagh, Ellora, Ajanta etc. but also in various temples in South India. It looks there were reasons behind the choice of such that limited scale of pigments in Indian murals. The action of time and other alkalies on colour also puts restrain on the artists to this ceiling. These colours have also been mentioned in *Silparatna*. *Manasollasa* also mention the use of red, green and blue of various shades.

The painter refined his technique during the medieval period and started using mixed colours also to bring about the desired tonal effect. However the classification of pigments continued to be the same comprising natural minerals and mixed colours. Vegetable colorants were also found used in paintings. Lacs and dyes were used generally late. In the 11th century AD we have much less information with regard to use of type of pigments in murals. However, palm leaf, wood, paper, paintings, Tankhas paintings as carrier started to be used. Some of the these were analysed by the author and this reveals the continuity of usage of similar pigments in addition to fewer vegetable extracts as colorant particularly in case of illuminated manuscripts as follows:

(A) Palm-leaf illustrated manuscript of *Panchraksha-sutra*,12th century AD.

1.	Support	-	Palm leaf		
2.	Ground	-	Kaolin		
3.	Binding	-	Medium-gum		
4.	Pigments	-	Blue-Ultramarine		
			Yellow	-	Ochre yellow
			Red	-	Haematite
			Green	-	Terra-verte
			Black	-	Lamp-black

(B) The Thanjavur paintings belonging to 12 and 13th century AD were analysed by Dr. Paramashevan and reports were published in technical studies in the field of fine arts and these are as follows:

1.	White	-	Line-White
2.	Black	-	wood charcoal/lamp black
3.	Blue	-	Ultramarine
4.	Yellow	-	ochre
5.	Green	-	Terraverte
6.	Yellowish	-	Ultramarine/Yellow ochre
7.	Light blue	-	Ultramarine with like to tone down
8.	Bluish green	-	Ultramarine/Terraverte
9.	Flesh	-	Iron and calcium carbonate

(C) Material use in Cloth Paintings of 14th and 15th century AD.

Satrunjaiya-Pata

Period	14th century AD		
Support	Cotton cloth		
Ground	Kaolin		
Binding Medium	Starch		
Pigments	1. Red	-	Vermillion
	2. Blue	-	Ultramarine
	3. Brown	-	Iron Oxide
	4. Green	-	Terraverte
	5. Black	-	Charcoal Black
	6. Golden	-	Gold in Powder form
	7. White	-	Talc

(D) *Sikandra* the Pigments were analysed by Nagpal and he detected the following (Mugal):

1. Red - Mercuric sulfide
2. Blue - Ultramarine
3. Green - Lead Chromate plus Prussian-blue
4. Other green - Contains iron
5. Yellow - Gold leaf yellow-ochre

(E) *Saraswati Pata*

Period	15th century AD.
Support	Cotton
Filler & pigments	Kaolin, 1. Red - Vermilion 2. Blue - Ultramarine 3. Green - Terraverte 4. Yellow - Indian ochre 5. White - Talc 6. Black - Carbon black 7. Golden - Gold
Medium	Gum

(F) Scientific investigation of *Jain Kalpa Sutra*

Period	15th century AD.
Support	Paper
Pigments	1. Golden - Gold in powder form. 2. Red - Vermilion 3. Black - Carbon black 4. Blue - Ultramarine blue

	5. Yellow	-	Yellow ochre
	6. Violet	-	Red madder

(G) Wall paintings from Rang Mahal, Chamba.

Period	18th century Murals		
Support	Wall		
Pigments	1. White	-	Chalk
	2. Black	-	Carbon black
	3. Green	-	Malachite green and chrysocolla
	4. Blue	-	Indigo
	5. Blue	-	Ultramarine
	6. Red	-	Indian red
	7. Yellow	-	Yellow ochre

(H) Wooden polychromes of 19th century—A scientific study.

Support	Wood		
Pigments	1. Red	-	Vermilion
	2. Blue	-	Ultramarine, Prussian blue
	3. Green	-	Verdigris
	4. White	-	Carbonate of lead and calcium
	5. Black	-	Carbon
	6. Red	-	Violet dye
	7. Yellow	-	Indian ochre
	8. Flesh colour	-	red lead and lime
	9. Shining	-	White tin metal

During the medieval and Mughal periods metallic compounds occuring as natural deposits like haematite, terraverte, as well as carbonate of copper were abundanty used as colorant materials. Some of these were used without any processing such as carbonate of copper, verdigris, orpiment, realgar, red lead, lead white, coloured earths, ochres and the red par excellence vermilion. Others in stone form were powdered, watered and then used as a pigment. Different tones were selected by various processes. Green tint was obtained from verdigris known as jangal or zangar, but a darker tone used in the background and vassi was obtained by blending indigo with orpiment. Moong green was obtained from moong. Later on, a larger number of vegetative natural occurring substances were tried and used specially for illustrated manuscripts. Among the other organic colouring matter, the madder, lac dye, cochineal red (1518), kirmis, and a dye obtained from coccus Indicus, an insect much found in Persia were all in use. Among the yellow, Indian peori an organic extract prepared mostly in Bengal from the urine of cows that fed on mango leaves was found in use. The colouring matter is principally magnesium or calcium, salt of exanthic acid. Another yellow was the extract of dhak flowers, also known as makli-peori.

In the 19th and 20th century AD, we encounter hundreds of new dyes when Perkin invented the methods for preparation of dyes. Earlier Diesback prepared Prussian blue in 18th century AD and in 19th century AD, we have lithopone. Rajasthani painters used similar pigments as Mughals. The dyes of animal origin used were:

1. Cochineal-red from small cactus eating insect, giving Carmine dyes of (C22 H CO13).

2. Ratanjot is a part of vegetative growth from family Borginaceae.
3. Saffron—From flowers of plant crocus asavitus.
4. Turmeric—Oleo resin.
5. Orchil—From roceella.
6. Riboflavin—Colouring matter.
7. Catechin—Brown colour from acacia Arabica.
8. Madder-Pinkish violet.
9. Chlorophyll—Green pigment.
10. Carmines—Reddish colour etc.
11. Lac—Pigments.

Problems

Since our country is located in a moonson rain forest type of climate, we have rapid deterioration on account of bio-chemico physical factors. The cumulative effects of humidity, temperature, pollution and particulate matter play their own part in degrading murals. The general deterioration is as follows:

1. Darkening of the surface accompanied by abrasions of surface
2. Fungus growth
3. Flaking/cupping of layers in a mural
4. Fading of colour due to light
5. Disintegration of binding medium
6. Cracks and pulverization

However some specific examples where serious difficulties arose are as follows:

1. Problems of dyes belonging to Bengal school: A large number of dyes have been used, particularly

yellow dyes which pose really serious problems. These are affected by water, alcohol, and several other organic solvents. This is difficult to be fixed up with usual preservatives. Several protective layers of PVA did not prove effective. Now we have to determine the nature of the dye.

2. Development of charring effect arose in case of Deccani and Western schools of paintings particularly in green pigments. It grows to such an extent that only a hole is left ultimately to what was once green. About 60 samples have been analysed. It is found to be verdigris. What is the actual chemical mechanism involved is not well understood. However, it is suggested that the probably sulfurous/ sulphuric acids may be the ultimate agency bringing about charring in cellulose. The problem is how to neutralize and make this tendency harmless.

3. In some other cases, another dreadful chemical reaction noted was in the case of red pigment. It was analysed and found to be vermilion, a beautiful bright red pigment gradually and slowly turning black. Its causes and cure have to be found out. Probably the alternation from cinnabar to metacinnabar, a black variety is taking place but whether it is due to chemical change or otherwise is not well understood. Further investigation is required.

4. Flaking in case of white pigments is another serious problem. On analysis of white pigment, it was detected to be zinc white which shows this type of tendency to a maximum.

5. Very recently while examining a few murals from Central Asia, a violet pigment was noted which was somewhat intriguing as no mention has been made

of such a pigment. On analysis it was found to contain lead. (Sir Aurel Stein mentioned that lead has been used as a white pigment). To remove or to convert this violet into white is another serious problem for which a remedy is yet to be found.

6. These are the few remarks on the pigments and their problems and I feel that probably future will come to our aid in finding a solution to save our cultural heritage.

Notes on Colour

1. In the medieval Sanskrit text *Manasollasa* (II, I, p. 157), crude cinnabar is mentioned as one of the red colours. The *Jaina-Chitra Kalpadruma* (I, pp. 45, 119) describes in detail the method of extracting red colour from crude cinnabar.

2. Ochre brown has not been mentioned as a simple colour in the Indian texts on paintings. *Manasollasa* (II, pp. 158-164) gives a list of mixed colours, one of which is brown colour, prepared by mixing lamp black with red ochre.

   A number of mixed colours are mentioned in a list obtained from the folio of an old MSS. in the possession of Mr. Marilal Lakshmichand Pande (*Jain-Chitra Kapadruma*, p. 47, fn. 63). One of the colours described is muddy brown (argaja) prepared by mixing zinc white and mango green in the proportion of 4:1.

   In another list of mixed colours, obtained by Mr. Sarabhai Nawab from some paper manuscript (Moti Chandra: *Jain Miniature Paintings from Western India*, Ahmedabad, 1949, p.87), there is mention of a dark body colour (*samalo rang*) made by mixing cinnabar zinc white and lamp black.

3. Sanskrit texts do not mention green as a separate colour. It was obtained by mixing several colours (Moti Chandra :

Jain Miniature Paintings from Western India, p.83).

Terraverte green, however, is used as separate colour in Ajanta paintings of Cave No. XVI and Ellora (Paramashevan-Technique of the paintings process in Cave Temple at Ajanta, *Ann. Rep. Archl. Dept. of H.E.H. Nizam's Dominion*, 1939, p. 29; Technique of the paintings process in the cave temple at Ellora, p. 38).

It is interesting to find terraverte green used in cloth painting as early as c. 1400 A.D.

Charcoal has not been mentioned as a pigment in any text. Lamp black has been mentioned as the only black pigment in the *Manasollasa* (II, 1, 157). *Silparatna* (*Chitralakshna* SS, 47-52) describes the method of preparing lamp black. This text also describes a black pigment obtained from a certain mineral (antimony?).

4. Gold leaves were used for decorating the stucco images and stupas in Gandhara as early as Ist-2nd centuries AD. Use of gold is not known in the wall paintings of Ajanta and Ellora. The *Vishnudharmottara Purana* (III, p. 40) mentions gold as one of the colours. Detailed processes of preparing gold powder are given in the *Manasollasa* (II, I, pp. 171, 177) and the *Silparatna* (*Chitralakshna* SSS-123-130). The latter text also describes the method of applying gold leaf to paintings.

   It appears that the use of gold paintings was reintroduced in India near about the middle of 14th century AD due to the influence of Persian paintings.

5. The *Manasollasa* (II, 1, p.139) mentions *naga* which may have been kaolin or gypsum, as a white used for plastering the wall before painting.

   The *Silparatna* (*Chitralakshna*, SS. 28-29) mentions burnt conch-shell and white earth used as priming material.

6. The *Silparatna* (*Chitralakshna*, S.29, SS. 51-52, S. 122, S.133) mentions exudations of the kapittha and him as astringents for tempering the colours. In the Jain

literature (*Jaina-Chitra Kalpadruma*, 1, p.42) the gums of nim, catechu and gum arabic are mentioned as binding media for lamp black.

The *Vishnudharmottara Purana* (Tr. by Dr. Stella Kramrisch. p. 51) mentions the use of exudation of the Sindura tree (Grislea Tomentosa) as an astringent for tempering the colours.

6

Management of Bhimbetka and Adamgarh

B.M. Pande

MY first exposure to rock art was way back in November 1959 when as a student of the School of Archaeology of the Archaeological Survey of India, I had an occasion to visit the rock shelters at Adamgarh on the outskirts of Hoshangabad in Madhya Pradesh. Later, while participating in the excavation at Burzahom, a neolithic site in Jammu and Kashmir, we found two stone slabs, one of which contained a hunting scene and the other had what has been identified as 'tectiform'. These two slabs containing engravings are, in my view, of particular importance since these have been found from stratified neolithic levels.

It was, however, on 6 December 1977 that I visited Bhimbetka in district Raisen, Madhya Pradesh for the first time from the point of view of conservation, preservation and maintenance of rock shelters. Interestingly enough, I found Prof. V.S. Wakankar, the discoverer there itself moving about all by himself. Subsequently, I made several visits to Bhimbetka as well as other rock shelters in and around Bhopal, at

Chiklod and those in the vicinity of the Siva temple at Bhojpur, the ones near the Raisen Fort in the hill range known as Hathitola and Ram Chhajja, the rock shelters at Talpura in tehsil Budhni, district Sehore, etc. Based on my several visits to these rock shelter sites and being entrusted with the responsibility we had to devise measures and initiate steps for their preservation. While recounting the measures that we adopted, which may appear to be rather simple and commonplace, I would be touching upon the problems that are usually confronted with in regard to conservation, preservation and maintenance of these sites. This narration is thus based on the experience about sites in Madhya Pradesh, particularly the ones which I mentioned in the beginning, i.e., Adamgarh, Bhimbetka, Bhopal, Raisen, Chiklod, Talpura, etc.

Of these sites, only the rock shelters at Adamgarh near Hoshangabad had then been declared as protected monuments by the ASI while steps had been initiated to declare the rock shelters at Bhimbetka and others as protected monuments. Due to the vast area in which these rock shelters are spread over and because of their location in forest area, problems were being faced even in regard to their protection. These problems were (a) mapping and plotting of individual rock shelters, and (b) maintaining coordination with the Forest authorities in regard to the information relating to revenue data. Coupled with this was the problem of evolving proper and intelligible system of numbering of individual as well as clusters of rock shelters. Before I go into the details, I would like to begin with the types of problems that we were confronted with.

Most, if not all sites containing rock art cover a vast area and are located in jungles or forests barring the ones in and around Bhopal or the Adamgarh rock shelters which are in close vicinity of a town. The problems about these sites also vary. Thus, for instance, the rock shelters at Adamgarh are located on the outskirts of Hoshangabad town and are close to the highway. At the time of my first visit to Hoshangabad, it was noticed that the area containing the rock shelters—even though it was homogeneous—had not been fenced even after demarcation. There was no one to regulate entry into the area and the rock shelters were being used by shepherds as well as undesirable elements from the town who found these as a safe haven for their activities. The rock shelters had also been vandalised by way of scribbling or application of oil paint over the surface of the rock shelters, in very many cases over the paintings as well. Of course, vandalism of ancient monuments is a feature not necessarily restricted to monuments or sites which are located in or close to a city. Besides, the area around the rock shelters had also been denuded of vegetation and there hardly existed any tree. As a result, during summer months in particular when wind was blowing, sand and tiny stone particles were causing abrasion to the painted surface of the rock shelters.

One of the first steps that we took was to have the entire area enclosed by barbed-wire fencing with access providing through a turnstile gate. Fencing definitely resulted in overall improvement of the area by way of checking entry of cattle. Consequently, we also took steps for planting trees within the fenced area and drew up a scheme for turning of the surrounding area so that the problem of abrasion by stone particles is checked and contained. I have not been able to visit Adamgarh subsequently in recent years. While we had suggested removal of oil paint applied on the surface of the original paintings, I am not in a position to say what chemicals could be used. Perhaps our colleagues who are specialists in this area would be in a better position to throw light on this.

The rock shelters at Bhimbetka presented a much more difficult situation due to several reasons. These rock shelters are located over a very large area with each cluster of rock shelters forming almost a unit, apart from individual rock shelters. However, the fact that these rock shelters are located in a forest area, parts of which are difficult of access, posed certain problems. At the time of our visit in December 1977, the rock shelters had not been declared as protected monuments. The area had also not been properly surveyed nor had the rock shelters been plotted except for their broad classification. The rock shelters at Bhimbetka (and Lakhajuar) had been divided into eight groups, Nos. I to VIII; each group was further subdivided into clusters of rock shelters A, B, C, etc. and each rock shelter within a cluster as well as the individual rock shelters were given a running number 1, 2, 3, etc. Thus each rock shelter was given a three-tiered number, for example III F - 23. This system of numbering was devised and followed by Prof. V.S. Wakankar as well as by Prof. V.N. Misra of the Deccan College. However, the University of Sagar had also adopted their own system of numbering the rock shelters which they had put on the rock shelters using black paint. To add to the confusion, the State Department of Archaeology and Museums, Madhya Pradesh, had also adopted their own numbering system. This incongruency could also be seen in the rock shelters in the Shamala Hills as well as those at Dharampuri in Bhopal. Thus, for example, in one of the rock shelters, three numbers namely III-A 25, BB-10 and B 12 have been simultaneously used causing much confusion. Unfortunately, in their zeal, all the three agencies had left their mark by using oil paint for writing the numbers.

I am mentioning these facts only to underscore the need for a coordinated approach by different agencies in this matter so that there is no scope for any confusion. In fact, the numbering or classification of the rock-shelter sites is intimately connected with their documentation. Now that the IGNCA has taken the lead in regard to rock art, I would suggest that it evolves a system which could be adopted by all agencies.

One of the steps that we took up simultaneously along with the survey of rock shelters as a prerequisite to their protection, was to provide approach to the main group of rock shelters. While the work of making a motorable road up to the main group was already in progress, nothing had been done by way of approach paths to the rock shelters. As a prerequisite to their better maintenance and as a facility for the visitors, approach paths leading to rock shelters Nos. III F-13, III F-16, II F-23, III F-21, III F-33 and the sites given subsequently named Pisacha Rock, Zoo Rock (III C-29, III C-21, III C-19 and III C-9) were provided. These approach paths were unobtrusive and not more than a metre and a half in width with a row of stones on either side of the path. It was ensured that the path was periodically cleared of growth of vegetation and the stones on either side were duly given coat of limewash from time to time. A general cultural notice board containing basic information in Hindi and English about the site was also placed near the entrance to the complex.

The specific problems regarding preservation and conservation at Bhimbetka that needed urgent attention were many. The first problem was about the trench which had been excavated by the Deccan College, Pune, in rock-shelter no. BTK F-23. Since this represented (then) the only excavated palaeolithic trench in the country, it was decided to preserve it in the best possible manner. This involved clearance of stones which had fallen inside the trench, checking ingress of water into it from the northern side along the face of the rock-shelter as well as from the sides of the trench. The steps taken for the purpose are as follows. First, a nearly 80 cm high rubble wall and of the same width was built utilizing the stones available in the area all along the excavated trench with the gradient towards the outer side. Only mud mortar was used in its construction and the top was covered with earth. All along the sides of the wall, shallow drains were provided for draining out of the water. At the point where the wall was abutting against the rock shelter, its height was raised to about 2 metres with proper slope towards the outer side so as to divert the flow of water from the top of the rock shelter and away from the excavated trench.

The other and more serious problem that we tried to tackle was about water flowing in from the sides of the rock shelter or seepage of water through crevices and fissures in the rock itself. These crevices and fissures were getting enlarged due to water seeping through these fissures and was adversely affecting the paintings. It was, therefore, decided to have the tree roots taken out and the fissures filled with earth and finally sealed with cement lime mortar. In my view, it is necessary to examine the upper portions of the rock shelters containing paintings in order to indentify, locate and seal the cracks and fissures before further damage is caused to paintings due to the flow of water. The paintings on the rock shelters, exposed as these are to weather and water, require urgent attention. I am not in a position to comment on or suggest methods for their chemical preservation about which itself I have my own reservations. However, one of the measures that could be tried is to make shallow channels along the top of the rock shelter close to the edge of the rock shelters so that flow of water inside into the rock face is either reduced or stopped.

The other problem that is equally grave is exfoliation resulting in flaking of the rock. I am not in a position to suggest any solution to this either.

At the same time, I would like to mention that use of any chemicals whether for cleaning and preservation of rock paintings or for checking the flaking of rock due to exfoliation requires to be carefully considered. I do not know if it is possible to replicate in a laboratory the various factors and processes that affect paintings in their natural surroundings and evolve suitable methods involving use of chemicals and their long term effect on them.

Finally, I may mention the man-made problems of deforestation, quarrying, use of material from rock-art sites to be used as ballast for roads, vandalism and conversion of rock-art sites into temples, shrines or their use even for residential purposes. The best (or the worst) example of the latter is at Bhimbetka where a large rock shelter has been turned into a temple or the group of rock-shelters at Bhopal which have been converted into a temple known as the Gupha Mandir. Of course, one could see evidence of rock shelters being used in subsequent periods for different purposes at several sites such as those near Dharampuri in Bhopal overlooking the Bhadbhada, or at Talpura where exist dry stone masonry platforms identical to the early historical stupa complex.

Reference

1. R.V. Joshi, *Stone Age Cultures of Central India (Report on the Excavations of Rock-shelters at Adamgarh, Madhya Pradesh)*, Deccan College Post-graduate and Research Institute, Poona, 1978.

7

Conservation and Management of Rock Art Sites

Bansi Lal Malla

ROCK ART is a precious cultural heritage of mankind. It is reported throughout the world and is widespread in India also. The rock paintings are considered as one of the fine arts practised by Early man to decorate the cave shelters. According to *Vishnudharmottara* (IIIrd Khanda), the practice of painting is the chief of all arts in this world. Perhaps, prehistoric people produced it for ceremonial and other purposes which we may never fully understand and appreciate. The preservation of this art is very necessary owing to the rapid rate of destruction caused by an unaware society.

Damaging Agencies

The ecological disturbances and problems of bio-deterioration are creating havoc in the preservation of rock art. Growth of micro-organisms like algae, fungi and bacteria results into dark stains. The other damaging agencies include fly marks, pigeons and lizards droppings, accumulation of dust and smoke due to alternate hydration and dehydration, oxidation of bonding material, etc. In the absence of adequate stalagmitic basaltic rocks, colour mutation due to action of water-borne chemicals, and because of constant superimposition of painted layers, it has been difficult to either preserve or date the paintings in the open rock shelters.

Threat from vandalism and tourism to the rock art sites is also noticed for many decades. The sites which have high profile. This human vandalism not only indicates lack of sensitivity and knowledge but also an alienation from the human family. The increasing pressure from tourism as well as fundamental problems of weathering and of the impact of vegetation and stock, indicate that there is an urgent need for conservation and management of Indian rock art sites.

Site Surveys

The site surveys and detailed mapping should be taken up at first instance as these can provide us new knowledge including details of their condition and source of actual and potential threat to the sites. In fact, the consideration of conservational problems should be worked out by a team of experts from different concerned fields.

In some cases, detailed recording may be the only way to conserve imagery, especially where it is degraded or where sites are threatened. The contents of rock paintings being so deep and abstruse need more meticulous investigation so that more accurate data can be obtained. Therefore, high scientific and technological methods of shooting, copying, colour mapping, close shotting, drawing, etc. should be used for recording and computerising the rock paintings.

Site Protection

Several rock painting sites have been designated by the Archaeological Survey of India as the 'government protected sites'. Perhaps no unified planning can be made as these sites as they are protected dispersedly and could not be joined and protected in a large range. In order to arrange integrally, a complete protected area of the site should be located. If possible, fencing of all major rock art sites should be taken up as it can be effective in keeping animals away from the imagery in rock shelters, because they also damage paintings by rubbing against paintings or licking them with salts from the walls. But it may produce further problems within a fenced area. It can result in build-up of heavy vegetation which might have disastrous impact upon rock paintings. Therefore, it is necessary to control vegetation growth and to prevent unnecessary fuel build-up within fenced sites.

The felling of trees must be forbidden in those protected areas where in the past decades the woods have become rare and the paintings once hidden in these woods got exposed to sunlight, wind and rain, and resulted into the quickened damage of rock paintings. It should be attempted to restore ecological environment by way of planting trees wherever woods are rare.

In the protected areas or in its vicinity, no factories should be allowed to build up, especially those discharging harmful gases and waste water, in order to stop the source of pollution and keep the environment clean.

It is encouraging to see that a few rock art site are included in the World Heritage List and converted into National Parks to protect and preserve the rock paintings as well as ecological balance of the area. At present, an attempt is being made to include Bhimbetka in the list.

Sometimes researchers themselves cause damage by sprinkling water on these figures to make them bright under reflection for study. This should be condemned and stopped at once. We should also condemn the practice of application of chalk or any such secondary thing to enhance petroglyphs because it can create the chances of damaging rock art. It may further create problems for future research, i.e., dating etc.

Site Restoration

Mud-nests made by mud-wasps and birds, besides salt deposits, are some typical problems affecting most of the rock art sites. If they are removed and treated timely, the paintings can be saved from any damage.

The surface of the cliffs of different rock shelters is usually found uneven and in some cases has cracks. Water sometimes penetrates through these cracks and results into the peel off, and even fall of large wall blocks. It is advised to plug the cracks which occur in the rock paintings, and those rock blocks which are prone to fall should be glued to the wall by filling organic high molecular material.

Some cliffs are almost perpendicular to the ground, having no projections in the upper part and in such cases paintings often suffered from rain, weathering and erosion. To keep off rain etc., roofs can be put up as soon as possible for this part of rock painting. The erosion of rock painting may also be stopped by making small water drains.

Because of hot climate, damp air and strong

sunlight in most parts of India, the colour of rock paintings has faded. The paintings which are covered by aqueous carbonate are believed to preserve their original colour. Similar method of spray transparent chemical membrance on the exposed paintings may help in preserving the rock paintings. However, these measures should be tested on a small scale under the direction of experts concerning the field.

Visitor's Management

The biggest threat to the rock painting seems to be from the increasing number of visitors. This necessitate a careful consideration of visitor's management. Restricted access combined with guided tours can prove beneficial for the protection of rock art as well as for the education of visitors. Visitors can be controlled less intrusively by the use of, firstly, structures which physically guide rock pictures and, secondly, well by researched and carefully presented information. It is generally seen that sites giving the appearance of being actively managed are less likely to be vandalised.

Besides, audio-visual aids which include leaflets, placed at the sites or at the nearby visitor's centres, can provide information and enhance protection. More informative signs, especially those interpreting imagery paintings, are appreciated by visitors.

It is necessary to provide a general educational programme for the public to develop an awareness of the responsibility towards preservation of our cultural heritage. This goal may be achieved by organising exhibitions, lectures with colour slides, video films and group discussions with the public. It will also require personal involvement of rock art researchers.

Similarly, a simple sign providing the site name,

prescribing the code of behaviour and listing penalties for offence against the law can also prove beneficial.

The visitors book too can half monitor visitation impact and contribute significantly to the site protection.

Conclusion

Appropriate visitor management can reduce the chances of vandalism, obviate inadvertent damage to rock art, lessen the impact of visitation upon site environs, and enhance visitor appreciation of rock imagery. But his alone will not do much. The provisions for policing/ monitoring of sites or exclusion of visitation, and the will of the relevant government authority to exercise its legal powers, must be invoked to effectively manage the sites and combat vandalism. In India, there are already legislations for the protection of cultural heritage sites but they need to be implemented strictly. If necessary, they should be modified or made tough enough to fulfil the desired goal.

Besides, insecticidal treatment for preservation of this primitive art for posterity seems to be an ultimate need of the archaeologists with the cooperation of research laboratories. At present, certain preservatives are used in different parts of the world to check moisture and rain water adversely affecting the rock paintings. It is imperative for scientists to evolve suitable preservatives and measures to protect the rock paintings of different climatic zones of India. Due to climatic factors the rock paintings have a distinct seasonal life of their own and that is yet to be studied. The variation in the visibility of the figures is an important point since it influences the recording and interpretation of a panel. The study of mechanisms of the exchange between the rock and the external environment from geological, climatological and hydrological viewpoints, in order to explain the present state of the painted wall and its evolution in future needs our immediate attention. Even pigment analysis is equally useful for conservation studies to detect salt traces, etc.

The National Research Laoratary for Conservation, Indian National Trust for Art and Cultural Heritage (NRLC, INTACH), Archaeological Survey of India and State Archaeological Departments can play an important role for taking extensive protective measures to save rock paintings. These departments should be equipped with special staff having expertise in the field, and also be provided with special funds to achieve this goal. It is time to realise and meet our responsibility for preservation and further study of rock art as being an important part of our proud cultural heritage. In conservation techniques we may have the benefit of experience of specialists of other countries. Regarding this, the IGNCA has already initiated a joint venture with France for the study and conservation of rock art, started in the year 1993. The study at present is going on in the right direction.

References

1. Agrawal, O.P. (Ed.). 1989. *Wall Painting of India—A Historical Perspective*. INTACH Conservation Centre, Lucknow.
2. Godwin, Luke. 1992. Carve your name with pride? Visitor behaviour of Blacks Palace art site complex, Central Queensland Highlands. *Rock Art Research:* 9(2).
3. Kumar, G. 1990. New dimensions in purakala study. *Purakala:* 1(1).

4. Morwood, M.J. & Kaiser Glass, Y. 1991. The use of graffiti in the monitoring of community attitude towards aboriginal rock art. *Rock Art Research:* 8(2).
5. Ward, Graeme K. 1993. Conservation of rock imagery in Australia: Funding support, protection projects and related research. *Rock Art Research*: 10(1).

8

The Cultural Dimension of Rock Art

Baidyanath Saraswati

ROCK ART, in one sense, is an orphan. Those who produced it are no longer alive to defend their works or world-view. But there are cultures such as India where the primal vision persists, and there are also places such as Australia and Africa where rock art is still a living pursuit. These traditions may give a clue to the original datum of rock art, as also its meaning and purpose.

Explanation in rock art studies is confined largely to innatism or essentialism ("Art for art's sake") and functionalism. Radical or Marxist anthropologists may draw upon the socio-economic levels of hunter-gatherer societies. There is an increasing wealth of evidence concerning interdependence between infrastructure and superstructure. More often than not, the ideological superstructure remains intact while the economic infrastructure is irreversably altered.

It is not my intention to point out the inadequacies of these theoretical positions. But, I wish to emphasize that cultural conception of time and history is diverse.

In some cultures such as Chinese, there is no formal codification of temporal dimensions—past, present, future— in a system of verbal tenses. The Indian conception of time is described as the interiorization and transcending of time. Considering the diversity of form and concept, there is no good reason to restrict the understanding of rock art in terms of linear time, marking it out by fixed points of time in history. The same view can be taken with regard to assumptions and explanations in rock art. The fundamental approach of the IGNCA in all its work is multi-layering, and multi-meaning within the systemic cultural whole. In one of her recent writings Dr. Kapila Vatsyayan has pointed out, "The interpenetration of levels of meaning within a concept and between concepts will have the fineness of a sharp needle and the fluidity of a drop of water or oil or an absorbent surface". Thus the process of threading the needle and the expansion of the point, the drop, the *bindu*, and thus the essensence of the explanation in many if not all domains of rock art can be identified.

Cultural Engineering

The rock art sites conservation is bound to both natural and cultural factors. I shall point out very briefly to the latter aspect.

Anthropologists and archaeologists claim that authors of rock art were hunter-gatherer and hence some of them say that rock art sites are the cultural property of the contemporary aborigines. Let us admit that very little is known about the cultural context of rock art. But the claim that rock art is peculiar to the hunter-gatherer is untenable. What it might suggest is that the artists of rock art were not individually inspired; they were responding to a collective cognitive system. The more substantive objection to the theory of the hunter-gatherer rock art comes from the ethnography of art itself. The motifs of rock art persist almost everywhere in rural India. No drastic break exists between the old belief and the new faith. It is clear that amidst the tidal waves of culture, basic elements of the old tradition were duly incorporated in the new creation. Extending the anthropic principle of the arts and taking into account the diachronic-synchronic view of culture, a general theory of rock art can be propounded. The cultural wave that introduced the first art of humankind, depicting the primal vision, has left behind innumerable rock art sites scattered in many parts of the world. The new cultural wave abandoned the old site, but carried on the essentials of its artistic tradition to the new settlements. Thus rock art and folk art are genetically connected and functionally located in the same cultural context. Such a state of affairs lead to the conclusion that rock art sites are treasures common to all humankind and hence protection of this cultural heritage is the universal responsibility.

Unesco has adopted various conventions and recommendations concerning the protection of historical monuments. Rock art sites are not historical monuments of the kind Indonesia's Borobudur or India's Taj Mahal or Chinese' Tung Huang cave is. There is a need to evolve a new perspective and a new method for preserving the rock art sites. Considering the fact that these sites treasure the first human art whose artists are unknown and whose ownership is collective, a new method had to be found to give them a new lease of life, making them a part of the present and future development of human art and culture. Such method, I suggest, will require total involvement of the cultural community, development of the relevant cultural knowledge, and adoption of modern scientific techniques of preservation. The new method can be called "cultural engineering of rock art sites".

By "cultural engineering" of a monument, I mean preservation and restoration of cultural heritage not as a dead object or a broken structure but a living entity capable of illuminating eternal values of human creativity. Its approach is holistic. It takes us beyond the usual task of restoration of structures and preservation of historical purity. It activates a cultural process of renewal and perpetual development. Its policy and strategy consist in clarifying the cultural message, identifying the universal principles, enhancing the pride in tradition, and transmitting the experience of the arts at its primal level. An example of "cultural engineering of rock art sites" can be cited from Australia where the aborigines are the owners of the rock art sites. They do not consider the rock paintings to be the work of any human artist. They believe that the great design is worked out for them by their creation ancestors. But they think it is their responsibility to freshen up the colours of the rock paintings from time to time. In the process, the archaeological value is lost but cultural value is maintained. Rock art in Australia thus becomes a living tradition.

The key points of "cultural engineering" are: a) ordering of cultural identity; b) furtherance of authority and powers in decision-making process; c) restoration, maintenance and effective use of cultural heritage; d) cultivation of new ideas, new insights, and new knowledge gained through direct participation; and e) development of new sense of sharing organizational role and responsibility.

Finally, effective application of "cultural engineering or rock art sites" depends upon three factors : 1) the self-organizing ability of the cultural community, 2) the moral support of Unesco and other international agencies promoting cultural heritage, and 3) the financial contribution of the national government.

Cultural Policies

Before designing any policy and programme for rock art site management, the designers' would need, firstly, to know what is the value of rock art, and secondly, they would also need to clarify whose heritage it is. If the concern is merely to date the beginning of human history, rock art may seem irrelevant to the living population, the common man. If the purpose is to investigate features related to the art itself, rock art is a phenomenon of abiding interest and value. In either case, it is a record of primal vision of the universe, a heritage of the entire humanity and not merely the cultural property of the particular nation where it is found.

Rock art has been interpreted with different theoretical orientations-generally based on vague and misguided notions of "primitive mentality". Primitive man is denied of having "deepest aesthetic feelings" and "highest moral and intellectual speculations". Following the evolutionary approach-addressing the propositions about human cognitive development and the process of evolutionary emergence of language-"scientific" claims are made for the "origin of art". Such claims may be considered, and rightly so, as ethnocentric, Eurocentric, or astringently anthropocentric view. Without questioning the internationality of such a viewpoint, we may turn to the cosmocentric view of art that may not be generally shared, but there are good reasons to develop it within the framework of "normal science", the sacred science of nature and culture. There are five points to which I refer briefly:

1. Rock art is a living tradition in many parts of the Old World.
2. The text of the classical Indian theory of art is consistent with the context of what is known today as aboriginal art.
3. The cosmocentric view dominates the lifestyle in the Old World.
4. Rock art is the record of "universal" simple themes of illuminating experience. Here art and religion seem to have a juxtaposed association.
5. Authors of rock art and sages of the Upanisadic philosophy reveal the same experience of the cosmos and man's place in it. Both look at the universe as sacred artifact.

If this viewpoint is acceptable, the quest or the quarrel for original datum of rock art becomes clearly unreasonable. The importance of rock art is primarily the importance of what it signifies. As the first record of man's vision and experience of the cosmos, it is a kairological art on which all the arts are hung. As a place of illumination, rock art site is a sacred monument. As a fact of history, it is inseparable from the human race.

It is necessary to agree to the sacred nature of rock art sites for obvious reasons. With the widening of communication network, it is not possible any more to keep them away from the vandalism of tourists and professionals. If they are sacred monuments, the purpose and policy of their preservation must be totally different from those followed in the case of other historical structures.

Almost invariably, rock art sites have been associated with the aboriginal people. It has been suggested by a very distinguished rock art specialist that "Where rock art continues to play a traditional role in the belief system of an indigenous people, the indigenes remain the owners of the art, and the wishes, priorities and preferences of non-indigenes become subordinate". This may be true for aboriginal Australia, but not for India where such distinction is totally irrelevant. Ownership of rock art cannot be decided on narrow concerns. Rock art is the cultural property of all those who believe it to be true. The world of rock art is not static. It has extended beyond the rock caves and shelters. Its fundamental intuition, motifs and styles persist in what is known today as folk and tribal art. Any view associating rock art with a particular culture or a nation, is obviously incompatible with its guiding spirit. When authors of rock art produced their works they were not divided by cultures and nations. Collective ownership of rock art by the human race is unquestionable.

As a collective cultural heritage, rock art must be preserved and restored so that its value can be shown in many ways. Professional interest is limited to identification of stages in the evolution of human culture and hence the suggestion that rock art sites must be preserved in their original state.

Traditional cultures also claim attention, but for a different reason. For an Australian aboriginal painter, all life is one and he is a part of life, bound immutably within a great design worked out for him by his creation ancestors. Aborigines definitely do not consider rock paintings to be the original work of any human artist, though men have the responsibility to freshen up the colours from time to time. Thus, rock paintings reflect the relationship between people and the land, the spiritual world of the ancestral beings and the natural species and phenomena of the human world. If the message of ecology and culture interface is conveyed so clearly, effectively and widely we cannot allow these sacred monuments to return to dust. Keeping the rock-paintings in their original state is ultimately unimportant, because they are already subject to widespread vandalism which we cannot possibly stop. "Cultural engineering" seems to be the only method of conservation and preservation of rock art.

List of Contributors

M.C. Joshi

Archaeologist. Former Director General of Archaeological Survey of India; Member Secretary, IGNCA.
Address : IGNCA, Janpath, New Delhi - 110001.

B.B. Lal

Former Director (Conservation) in the Archaeological Survey of India.
Address : D-1/106, Satya Marg, Satya Sadan, Chanakyapuri, New Delhi.

B.L. Malla

Art-historian. Associated with Ādi-Dṛṣya Programme of IGNCA.
Address : IGNCA, Janpath, New Delhi - 110001.

B.M. Pande

Archaeologist and Former Director (Publications) in the Archaeological Survey of India.
Address : Y-81, Hauz Khas, New Delhi - 110016.

B.N. Saraswati

Anthropologist, UNESCO Professor in Cultural Development. Involved in experiments with multi-cultural approach to education.
Address : IGNCA, Janpath, New Delhi - 110001.

V.H. Sonawane

Director of Archaeology in the M.S. University, Vadodra. Address : 1/6, Vrindavan Estate, Pasabhai Patel Park, Race Course, Vadodra - 390015.

B.N. Tandon

Former Joint Director General (Conservation) in the Archaeological Survey of India.
Address : 174, Vigyan Vihar, Delhi - 110092.

1. Fragile nature of rocks developing cracks, Jhiri, Dist. Raisen, M.P.

2. Paintings exposed to direct sunlight, Jhiri

3. Impact of sunlight and bio-deterioration on paintings, Jhiri

4. Documentation of paintings by theodolite, Jhiri

5. Documentation of paintings by photographic & tracing method, Jhiri

6. Bio-deterioration impact on paintings, Bhimbetka, Dist. Raisen, M.P.

7. Bio-deterioration impact on paintings, Bhimbetka

8. Rock-paintings damaged by bio-deterioration, Kharwai, Dist. Raisen, M.P.

9. Impact of sunlight and rain on paintings, Pachmarhi, Dist. Hoshangabad, M.P.

Index